SQUASH
in a week

Rob Shay

Headway · Hodder & Stoughton

ACKNOWLEDGEMENTS

The authors and publishers would like to thank Roddy Paine for the photographs, and Hardlines for the artwork.

British Library Cataloguing in Publication Data
Shay, Rob
  Squash in a week. – (Sports in a week).
  1. Squash rackets
  I. Title   II. Series
  796.343

ISBN 0-340-53837-6

Colour origination by Colorcraft Ltd.
Typeset by Rowland Phototypesetting Ltd, Bury St Edmunds, Suffolk.
Printed in Hong Kong for Hodder and Stoughton Ltd, Mill Road, Dunton Green, Sevenoaks by Colorcraft Ltd.

CONTENTS

INTRODUCTION

Squash is the boom game of the past two decades, with more than three million people in Britain now playing regularly. It is a game of angles with a greater variety of stroke choice than other racket sports, such as badminton or tennis.

You may want to play to keep fit, to meet people, or you may simply enjoy the unique pleasures of a game which is called 'physical chess', the challenge of trying to win a game which requires determination, speed, skill, stamina and, above all, guile.

Squash will get you fit, but you need to be fit for squash. You need to be physically fit – if you're over forty and are not used to regular physical exercise, then start slowly and have a check up with your doctor first – and technically fit – you need to understand what squash is about, and how and when to play the basic shots.

The aim of this book is not only to show you the techniques of squash, but also to help you to learn by **observation**, and to improve by analysing and correcting your own technique.

On the first day, you will learn the basic racket skills and controls which will allow you to progress. Hitting the ball requires a sound technique, a technique which will work for all the basic squash shots.

Over the seven days of this book, you will learn the basics of the game: most importantly, how and where to hit the ball.

On each shot we will look at the basic stroke and look at ways of practising on your own or with a friend.

All the exercises are colour coded:

> Green : Beginners
> Blue : Intermediate
> Red : Advanced

Most of the exercises are aimed at beginners, but there is a selection of tougher exercises at the end of each section to use as you improve.

You will learn how to watch others, how to watch yourself, and how to measure your improvement. You will also learn how to assess your own shots.

Seven days is not long enough to master squash, but it is long enough to learn the rudiments of the game and to develop a level of competence which will help you understand the beauty of the game and how to get the most out of it.

But first you have to know where to begin . . .

STARTING OUT

Squash is a racket sport which takes place in a room 32 feet long, 21 feet wide and at least 15 feet high. The game is played by two players hitting the ball alternately, so that the ball strikes the front wall either directly or off a side or back wall.

Only one bounce is allowed on the floor after the ball has hit the front wall, but it may be volleyed.

What equipment do I need?

Squash is relatively cheap to play.

A metal squash racket costs as little as £15, and a wooden one is cheaper still. But if you are going to play regularly, it is better to choose a graphite racket, which will give you more power and cause less physical damage, through vibration, to your arm. A cheap graphite racket will cost as little as £30, and even the best ones will only cost £100. A squash ball will cost £1.50 or less, but more on that later.

Selecting a good pair of shoes is very important. Most leading manufacturers carry a specialist shoe in their range. A good squash shoe is light, but strong enough to stand more twisting and turning than a normal running shoe. A squash shoe must also have a light coloured rubber sole. Dark soles are banned by all clubs and centres because of the damage they do to the court floors.

Squash clothing is generally lighter and allows more movement than tennis gear. The rules of the game allow shorts or skirts of any colour, but only a pastel or white top.

Where can I play?

Squash is generally organised through commercial or members' clubs and, as a general rule, they would charge court fees of £4 to £5 per hour. If you do not want to incur the expense of actually joining a club to start with, most local authorities have squash courts in their sports centres.

If you are still unable to find a place to play, the sports governing body, the Squash Rackets Association, will have a full list of clubs in your area. They can be contacted at:

West Point
33–34 Warple Way
Acton, London
W3 0RQ
Telephone: 081-746 1616

The court

Squash has been likened to physical chess or snooker, and looking at the court you can see why.

Not only do you play to the front wall, as though facing a net in tennis and badminton, but you can use the side and back walls to keep the ball away from your opponent.

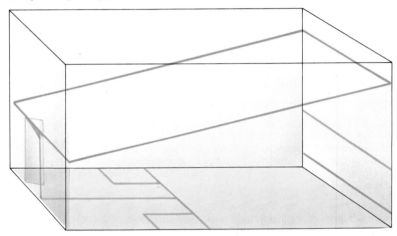

As we have already said, the game of squash takes place in a room 32 feet long by 21 feet wide. There are two important lines on the court – the **Out of Court** line and the **Tin** (shown in red on the diagram above). If the ball hits any wall above the Out of Court line, the striker loses the rally. Similarly, if it hits the front wall below the level of the Tin, the point is lost.

All the other lines (shown in green) are for service only. On service, the server must have one foot completely within the service box and the ball must hit above the cut line, over the short line, and on the opponent's side of the half court line.

Where the short line meets the half court line is the area known as the 'T'. This is central to the tactics of the game as we shall see later. For now, just remember that the 'T' is the area that you try to dominate, by returning to it after you have hit the ball and by keeping the ball as far away from it as possible.

The tools of the game

The squash ball

The first thing you will notice when you pick up a squash ball is the bounce – or rather the lack of it. Unlike the balls used in most sports, a squash ball is, as its name implies, 'squashy' and hardly bounces. But as it warms up in the course of play, so it bounces more.

As a beginner, you need a ball which bounces more than the standard match ball, because this makes it easier to hit. To help you choose the ball best suited to your standard of play, balls are colour-coded.

The standard ball for tournament play has a yellow dot on it, and although it is by far the most commonly used ball, it is not really suitable for beginners. The following chart will help you choose the correct one:

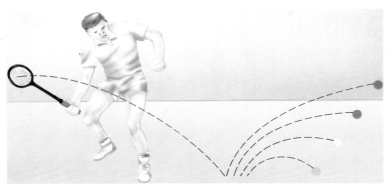

- o Blue dot: Absolute beginners and young children.
- o Red dot: Beginners and low grade players.
- o White dot: Moderate players and good players on a cold court.
- o Yellow dot: Good players.

The racket

Now the racket. A standard squash racket is 685mm (27 inches) long and has a width across the head of only 212mm (8.36 inches). It weighs less than 9 ounces, and so will feel a lot lighter in the hand than a tennis racket, but more substantial than a badminton racket. It is important to remember this when learning how to hit the ball. Squash has its own techniques which need to be learnt in order to get the most out of the game.

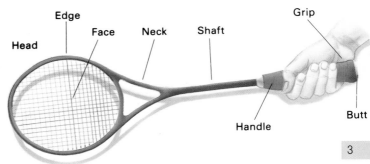

Technique

A good technique leads to better results – there is a way to hold the racket, to stand, to swing, to move and a point of contact with the ball which is better than the others because it leads to better, more consistent results with less effort.

If your technique is sound, you have the **potential** to play to a higher level than if your technique is flawed. So what are the basic techniques?

They can be split into four main areas:
(i)   The Grip;
(ii) The Swing;
(iii) Positioning; and
(iv) Movement.

Let's look at each one in turn:

The grip

Taking the shaft of the racket with your spare hand, point the racket head upwards and away from you. Now take the racket handle lightly in your playing hand, so that the 'V' formed between your thumb and forefinger sits over the inside edge of the racket as shown below.

Space your fingers along the shaft and keep your thumb down, wrapping it around the shaft.

The heel of the palm should rest near the end of the handle.

As a general rule, the grip stays the same for forehand and backhand shots.

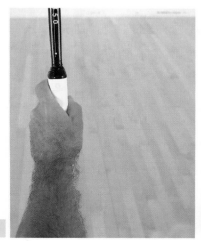 

Holding the racket wrongly affects the way you strike the ball, and will prevent you from playing to your full potential.

In particular, watch out for these three common faults;

'Clutching' the racket

Hold the racket firmly enough to control it, but not so firmly that you throttle it! If you hold it too tightly, you will lose control, particularly on the delicate shots.

Hold it as firmly as you would if you were writing. If you clutch a pen too hard, you cannot write properly. As with writing, to control a racket you need a sensitive grip so that you can 'feel' the racket head when you are hitting.

Remember, if you can see the whites of your knuckles, you are holding it too tightly!

The 'closed face'

Holding the racket too far round in your hand, so that the face of the racket is 'closed', is a common problem. Unless it is corrected early on, you will run into serious difficulty in the back corners, and have trouble clearing a ball hit down the side wall. For all the basic squash strokes the face should be 'open'.

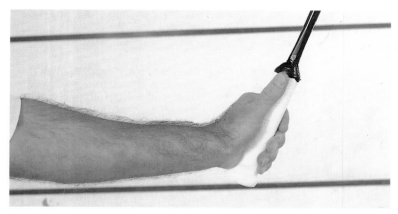

'Pushing' the backhand

As a beginner, you may find that you can control the backhand better by holding your thumb along the shaft and 'pushing' the racket. Unfortunately, this only works at a low level of squash and should be avoided, because it stops you from developing a genuine swing and proper control.

The swing

A squash swing is a smooth, throwing action.

On the forehand, this looks like a sidearm cricket throw, or the action you would use if you were skimming a stone across water. On the backhand, it is similar to throwing a frisbee.

The squash swing relies on a 'cocked' wrist action to be effective. It is often wrongly referred to as a wristy action.

Badminton players use a genuinely wristy action, or flick, to hit the shuttlecock, but this is not as effective with a heavier squash racket.

A floppy or 'broken' wrist will generate neither the power nor control which comes from a cocked wrist, as we shall see later.

Now take the racket to the top of the backswing, to start a forehand. With your elbow bent and your wrist cocked, swing smoothly through the ball, and let the racket come to rest in a similar position on the follow-through. Note that the swing starts with a 'square' formed by the racket, forearm and upper arm.

As you start the downswing, keep your wrist cocked, and start as though you were going to hit the ball with the butt of the racket, or the side of your hand. That keeps the racket in a dynamic position and allows you to generate controlled power at the point of impact.

Squash needs a firmer action and the forearm rather than wrist is used, as shown.

The racket should not be allowed to drop, as shown above.

At the end of the shot, the racket should come to rest in another 'square' at the top of the follow-through. Note that the racket face is slightly 'open', or facing upwards, at the point of impact. (See page 9.)

Note how the racket, forearm and upper arm form a 'square' at the top of the backswing. The wrist is cocked and body weight biased towards the leading foot. (Left foot for a right-hander, right for a left-hander.)

As the downswing starts, the wrist remains cocked and the arm swings down as though about to hit the ball with the butt of the racket. The square opens slightly, but the arm should not be allowed to stretch out fully, nor should the angle between racket and arm become a straight line. The racket face is open

At the point of impact, the wrist remains cocked. The racket face, still slightly open, hits firmly through the ball

The racket comes to rest forming another square at the end of the swing. Note that the racket face has stayed open throughout, giving control and depth to the shot. The 'closed' face (see page 5) will lead to less depth and more mistakes

Note the gentle swivelling movement of the shoulders in the illustration above. The shoulders should not be used to hit the ball, but should be opened as you take the racket back to give you a longer downswing. A long backswing gives you time to build up speed on the downswing without having to 'force' the shot.

Remember when you swing that there is someone else on the court with you. An excessive squash swing can be dangerous, particularly if you straighten your arm at the beginning or end of the shot.

The backhand swing follows a similar path.

Step in to play the shot facing the side wall. Your weight needs to be biased towards the leading foot, in this case your right leg (left for a left-hander). A square is again formed at the top of the backswing

As with the forehand, the shot starts as though you were going to hit the ball with the butt of your racket. The square opens but not fully. The racket face stays open throughout

The point of impact is about six inches in front of your front foot. The racket face is slightly open and your head should be steady, with your weight following in behind the shot

*Hit though the ball again, with the racket coming back
to rest in the square position*

The action owes more to golf than to badminton or tennis, because the main intention is to get controlled power with minimum effort.

Coaching tip – hold the racket with two fingers

To check that your swing is smooth, try holding the racket with just two fingers as shown. With the racket cradled against the ball of your hand and held lightly by your thumb and forefinger, swing the racket through an imaginary ball. This will give you some idea of where the power in the shot really comes from

Now try it with the ball. The swing should feel smooth, and you should hardly feel the ball on the strings. This tip can be used whenever your timing is wrong, or if you feel that you are trying too hard. A relaxed grip is essential.

11

BALL CONTROL AND THE DRIVE
Coaching tip – learning to watch

Watching and absorbing are the keys to learning any basic bodily skill. How do babies learn to walk? Not by reading the instruction manuals, nor by listening to a coach carefully explaining the subtleties of technique!

They watch, they absorb what they see, they imitate. Thus they learn.

In the same way, they learn to talk by listening to sounds and copying them.

Learn as a baby learns.

Watch better players, watch how they move and watch how they hit the ball. Most club players will confirm that their game improves just by watching a game at top level. Watching begets imitation, even if it is unconscious. Watch a top player and it will 'rub off' on you. This is the simplest and most effective way of learning at any level.

But watch your own game as well. Watch your swing in front of a mirror, compare it with the pictures in this book, and try to smooth out the creases and wrinkles.

Ball control

Let's get used to the feel of the racket, ball, and court with some basic exercises. Absolute beginners and juniors should start at the beginning, but if you have played racket sports before, you may find the first ones easy. Simple exercises will help to acquaint you with the length of the racket and the bounce of the ball.

That is the first stage of ball control.

Exercises for further practice

Now try to improve your ball control with these simple exercises:

- 1) Take the ball and bounce it to shoulder height on the open face of the racket. Starting gently, see if you can do it ten times (top left).

  Now hit the ball slightly higher, to head height, and repeat ten times.

- 2) Now turn the racket, and do it ten times on the reverse or backhand, side (top right). Do not change your grip.

3) Now alternate, backhand and forehand, and repeat ten times.

- 4) Standing sideways on, three metres from the front wall, drop the ball to the racket face and stroke it to the front wall (above). Try to do this ten times, letting the ball bounce between shots.

- 5) Now turn around and do the same with the backhand. If you have trouble starting the rally off, try throwing it off the side wall first, hitting it after the bounce.

13

- 6) When you can do this on both sides, try moving back a metre, and do ten shots on either side again. To get the ball back a little further, aim slightly higher on the front wall – above the level of the cut line.

Next, try the same exercise but on the volley, that is without letting the ball bounce (below).

Check your technique as you go along:

Is your grip correct?

Are your shoulders facing the side wall?

Are you far enough away from the ball to be able to hit it with your weight leaning forwards?

If you are right-handed, is your left foot forward on the forehand, and right foot forward on the backhand? (Vice-versa for a left-hander.)

Safety on the squash court

Due to the nature of the game, there are several dangers in playing squash which can be avoided with a few simple precautions:

1 Keep your eye on the ball at all times

A squash ball can do a lot of damage if it hits you, and most injuries happen with beginners. When the ball goes behind you, don't watch the front wall and wait for it to come back into view. You may feel it before you see it!

Even more dangerous is to let the ball go out of your field of vision, and then remember that you are supposed to be watching and turn to see it.

Note how the player on the 'T' watches his opponent striking the ball in the back corner. It makes the shot easier to read, he has a head start on moving to the next shot, and can take evasive action if the striker's shot is wayward

The player on the 'T' is waiting for the ball to come back into his field of vision. He cannot read the ball and runs the risk of being hit

Eye injuries are the most common serious injury amongst squash players. A squash ball is about the same size as the eyeball, and if the two should meet, the squash ball will usually come out of the encounter better off! Not only does the ball cause damage on impact, it creates a suction effect, which can damage the optic nerve. If you do get hit in the eye, go straight to hospital. The injury may seem slight at the time, but delayed damaged, such as a blurring of vision, may take place a few days later.

15

2 Keep a tight swing

A dangerous backswing

A dangerous follow-through

Remember when you play squash that your opponent is on the same side of the net as you. You are fighting to dominate the same central area of the court. Inevitably there will be a bit of bumping into each other, but don't use your racket as a weapon to create more space. Keep the racket up and your elbow bent, at the beginning and end of the swing. A straight arm backswing (shown top left) and an excessive follow-through (bottom left) are both dangerous, and should be cured at an early stage.

3 Don't crowd your opponent

You may be eager to move for the next shot, but let your opponent play first. He may play a deceptive change of direction, and if you are too close and misread it, there is a good chance of getting hit with the racket.

Crowding your opponent. This is dangerous for the person crowding both on the backswing and follow-through.

4 If there is a risk of physical danger, play a let

The rules of squash were written with safety in mind.

A **let** is played when a player is unable or unwilling to play because his or her opponent is impeding or is in the way, or if there is the danger of physical contact as in the first photo.

However, if your opponent obstructs a potentially winning shot, in a direct line to the front wall, as in the second photo then the striker can claim a **penalty stroke**.

Striker A has hit a loose shot to the middle of the court. Player A stops the rally because of the danger of striking Player B. Player B is not in a direct line to the front wall, so a let is played

Player B has hit the ball back to him- or herself. Player A cannot hit the ball in a direct line to the front wall (arc C) without endangering Player B. Penalty stroke to Player A

The rules governing lets and penalty strokes are fairly complicated (see the appendix for the full rules), but as a beginner, stick simply to the following guidelines:

(i) If there is any risk of collision or danger to a player, stop and play a let.

(ii) If you are in any doubt, play a let.

(iii) If the erring player is obstructing a potentially winning shot to the front wall, a penalty stroke is awarded to the striker.

Coaching tip – get used to the squash environment

Get used to the bounce of the ball, and the feel of the court.

As a beginner, you need to get used to the feel of the ball on the strings of the racket, the bounce of the ball and the squash court environment.

And not just as a beginner – even the best players need to familiarise themselves with the ball and the court and, above all, to feel comfortable. If you are about to play an important match, take a little time out to get your rhythm going, by hitting the ball back gently to yourself on both the forehand and the backhand – gently, not hard – this will set your mind and body in the groove for playing. Most players at some stage will know the feeling of arriving on court for a match, and sensing that they are not hitting the ball quite right. A gentle warm up, where you concentrate on getting a simple rhythm going, moving your feet and checking your position of address will eliminate this problem. Try it!

Drives

The primary shots in squash, the building blocks for a sound game, are the forehand and backhand drives.

But what makes a good drive?

A good drive has two dimensions which are vital to any tactical understanding of squash – **length** and **width**. What do they mean?

Length

A good length shot is one which puts your opponent in a difficult position at the back of the court. Ideally the ball should bounce between the back of the service box and the back wall. The ball may be hit high and softly, or it may be hit hard and low, but try to get enough depth on it to put your opponent under pressure.

The easiest place to hit a ball is just past the top of the bounce. To make life difficult for your opponent, that point ought to coincide with the back wall, so that he or she has to decide whether to take it before or after it reaches the back wall – and neither is an easy option!

When practising the drive, concentrate on hitting it high enough on the front wall to get length. As you get more and more control, start to go harder and lower.

One of the great mistakes in squash is to hit the ball hard rather than deep, with the result that you have less control, and you get tired more quickly!

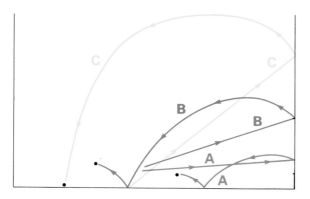

Look at the diagram. The higher a ball is hit on the front wall, the further it will travel. Balls A, B, and C are all hit at the same speed, but C will travel much further because of its higher trajectory. So, if you are not getting the ball to a good length, aim higher.

Width

A good width shot is one which is difficult to hit because it is close to the side wall. A shot which clings to the side wall is very difficult to hit, because there is much less control. Try to keep your straight drives within a foot of the wall, and, if hitting cross court, try to make the ball hit the side wall just beyond the back of the service box.

Former world champion Geoff Hunt, arguably the best striker of a squash ball in his prime, describes in his autobiography the basic disciplines which laid the foundations of his game:

'When I began squash as a boy, my father made me hit the ball along the side walls of a squash court for the first three months before he would allow me to attempt any other sort of shot. The object was to develop a good length, almost as a reflex action. I have been grateful for that grounding ever since.'

Hitting cross court

A deep cross court drive can be as effective as a straight one, but is far more risky. Furthermore, most beginners play the cross court automatically, when the straight shot is the better and safer shot to play.

A badly played cross court opens the court up for your opponent, and is probably the commonest mistake amongst beginners. Remember, when your body is screaming out for you to play a cross court, that is almost certainly the time to play it straight!

When you do play the cross court drive, aim to hit the opposite side wall near the back of the service box, as in the diagram below. But as a general rule, remember that it should not be played too often!

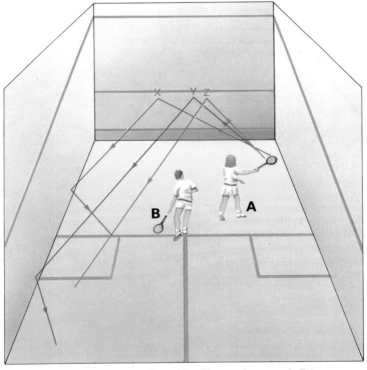

The cross court played by Figure A on path Z is not wide enough and will be cut off by Player B in the middle of the court. Path X is too wide and will come back to the middle off the side wall. Path Y is wide enough to get past Player B, and is also deep enough to finish in the back corner

Points to remember on the drive

(i) Keep your racket head up, with your wrist cocked at the top of your backswing.

(ii) Keep far enough away from the ball to be able to step into your shot.

(iii) The point of impact is just behind or in line with your knee on the forehand and just in front of your knee on the backhand.

(iv) Keep your head steady and your body balanced at the point of impact.

(v) Hit right through the ball, finishing with the racket high.

(vi) Aim to land the ball behind the services box.

Exercises for further practice

- 1) See how many forehand drives you can hit in successsion – they should land behind the short line and in the forehand half of the court. (Target A1) Then do the same on the backhand side. (Target A2)

- 2) When you can do ten in a row, reduce the size of the target, so that you have to keep the ball between the side of the service box and the wall (Target B1). Try for ten shots again and repeat on the backhand side (Target B2).

- 3) Next, give yourself a harder length target, hitting ten shots in succession behind the service box (Target C1).

  Repeat on the backhand side (Target C2).

- 4) Now give yourself a target of half the width of the service box, try for ten shots in a row (Target D1) and repeat on the backhand side (Target D2). You can mark your targets with chalk lines, and keep a record of your success on the personal assessment sheet which follows this section, so that you can measure your improvement.

  If you find that you are weaker on one side than the other, practise more on that side, rather than avoiding the weaker side.

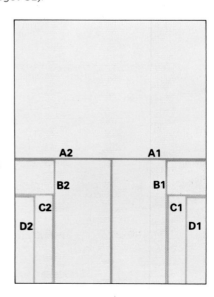

- 5) Starting from the service box, keep a rally going with each shot hit slightly shorter than the previous one, so that you take a step nearer the front wall with each successive step. When you get close to the front, start hitting the ball a little deeper so that on successive shots, you are moving one step back, until you are hitting a good length. Like many exercises in ball control, this is a very frustrating one when you first start!

- 6) The 'Figure-of-Eight' exercise. Starting from the 'T', hit a soft forehand drive to the opposite side of the front wall, about a foot from the corner. It will come back to your backhand, which you then hit similarly to the opposite front corner (see below). After a lot of practice, this exercise will help to iron out weaknesses in technique on the backhand or forehand. The forehand drive should finish where the backhand drive starts, and vice versa.

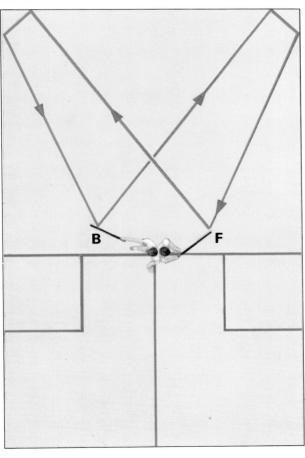

Your personal assessment

You can assess your improvement in these exercises by recording your scores on the assessment chart below.

When you can consistently hit Target A (see diagram on page 22) ten times in succession, move to target B, then C, and D. Practise your backhand as well as your forehand.

Exercise	Forehand/ Backhand	Day 1	Day 2	Day 3	Day 4	Day 5	Day 6	Day 7
1 Target A	FH							
	BH							
2 Target B	FH							
	BH							
3 Target C	FH							
	BH							
4 Target D	FH							
	BH							
5 *	FH							
	BH							
6 Fig-of-8	**							

*See how many times you can move to the front, then all the way to the back without making a mistake.
**When you get to ten shots, keep going – it helps you develop rhythm and is great for your concentration as well!

STARTING A RALLY – SERVICE AND SERVICE RETURN

Now that you can hit the ball, you can play **rallies** with your partner, or by yourself. A rally starts with a service, and a good service is one of the keys to good squash. Even more important is getting the service back; for every time you fail to return the ball, you lose a point. The service is the only time during the course of a rally when you have the ball in your hand and can do what you like with it, so don't waste it. Many people use the service simply as a way of starting the rally. But it can be used to pressurise your opponent from the first shot.

The rules of service

All the lines on a squash court, with the exception of the tin and the out-of-court line, are there only for service.

The server has one service, and must stay within the following boundaries:

1 The Service Box
The server must stand with one foot completely in the service box and serve to the opposite side of the court. You can put both feet in if you want, but one foot must be completely inside, without any part of it touching the red line before you strike the ball.

2 The Service Lines
The service must hit the front wall above the **cut line**, so that it bounces beyond the **short line**, and lands in the opposite half of the court, marked by the **half court line**.

The three serves shown by the coloured lines in the diagram below are all acceptable.

The server's options

A right-hander serving from the left box has many choices, but three most common options would be:

Path A: to hit a high lob serve, as described below;
Path B: to hit a lower, harder serve which should end up on a similar point on the side wall to A;
Path C: to hit down the other side or at, the receiver, to break up the rhythm.

Note that the ball is hit ⅔ to ¾ of the way across the front wall. A left-hander in the same position would aim much closer to the centre of the court.

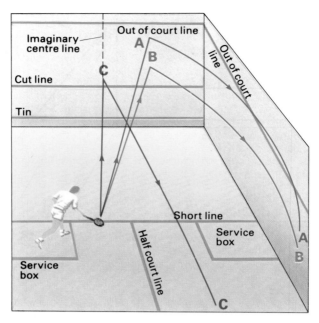

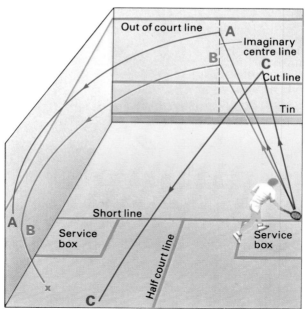

Those are the rules, but to make it as difficult as you can for your opponent, try to get the ball to reach the side wall and as near to the back wall as possible.

The most difficult service to return is the one which hits the side wall directly opposite the place you are waiting to receive it.

Opposite: From the right-hand box, the right-hander will aim near an imaginary line down the centre of the court, while the left-hander will aim 2/3 to 3/4 of the way across the court, to finish in the same place. This is because of the difference in the striking position

How to serve

There are many different ways of serving, so you need to find the one that best suits your game. It may be a high lobbing service, or it may be hard and low, but the principles involved are the same. Use the rules of the service to your advantage.

The rules say that you can serve from anywhere as long as one foot remains completely within the service box. The best place to stand is in the corner nearest to the centre of the court, so that you are well placed to step onto the 'T' when you have served.

Check your balance. Take your time. Look at your opponent's position. Aim at a spot on the side wall directly opposite where he or she is waiting for it. With wrist cocked, strike the ball well in front of your front foot.

Try to make the ball hit the side wall before your opponent can volley it. It is harder to judge a ball which is bouncing off the wall opposite you than to judge a ball coming straight off the front wall.

1 The lob service

The idea of a lob service is to pressurise your opponent with the ball's trajectory – the lob serve dips out of the lights at an awkward angle to hit and will die in the back of the court if allowed to bounce. To play it as a right-hander from the left-hand service box, start near the front of the box. Step into the shot, racket face open, and aim high onto the front wall.

Step into the shot so that at the end of serve you swing easily into position on the 'T'. Strike the ball in front of your front foot.

There is no need to throw the ball up high, just let it drop onto the racket, and stroke through it.

Depending on the speed you hit it at, aim to within a metre of the out-of-court line. The ball should hit the opposite side wall high up, and near to the back, so that if it is allowed to bounce it will hit the floor just before the back wall.

The path of the ball is shown as path 'A' in the photograph below.

PATH OF
RACKET

PATH OF
BALL

The lob service. Note the path of the racket, coming under the ball to achieve height on the front wall. The server is well placed to move straight to the 'T'

2 The standard service

The ball is struck more firmly than a lob service and takes a lower trajectory. Rather than coming underneath the ball and lifting it, throw the ball higher and strike it between waist and shoulder height. With an underhand service, you run the risk of hitting the ball either below the cut line, or out of court on the side wall.

Aim two to four feet above the cut line and, as with the lob service, aim to get the ball to hit the side wall just beyond the opposite service box.

The pace of the service can be varied from a semi-lob to a smash. The trajectory may vary, but ultimately you still want the same width – aim to hit the side wall just beyond the service box – and the same length with the ball dying in the back corner.

AREA OF
MAXIMUM
CONTROL

The hitting area for a standard service. A ball struck between the shoulder and hip area will be easier to control than one which is hit too high or too low

3 The surprise service

A hard service down the centre of the court is often an effective surprise tactic. It is best used when your opponent is too committed to receiving a shot on the side wall, or if he or she is simply getting your regular service back too easily.

If your opponent is weak in the air, in other words on the volley, aim the serve higher and deeper. Your target area increases against a player who is not that keen on taking the ball early.

Coaching tip – develop a service routine

Watch a top class tennis player serve. He or she will have a complicated routine which is repeated time and again. He or she may bounce the ball once or twenty times, but it is always the same ritual. A tennis player has 30 seconds between serves to prepare and a smaller target to hit. A squash target area may be large, but the benefits to be gained from serving with precision to a difficult part of the court are great.

Try to groove your action. To improve your consistency and accuracy, position yourself carefully in the same place and go through the same routine with every service.

At competition level in squash there is rarely a wining service, but a good, well considered service will put your opponent under pressure at the beginning of the rally and force errors.

If you are under pressure, your service will probably tense slightly, and may not touch the side wall. If this is happening you need to have an objective target to aim for. If you are tense, you will almost certainly be over cautious, play away from the out line and end up hitting an easy service.

Question: What do I do if my opponent can volley well, and is consistently killing my service?

Answer: Try varying the service more. Vary the pace, so that your opponent's return cannot get into a rhythm. Throw in the occasional hard service down the middle of the court. Many top players do this. At a top level, the chances of serving a winner are slim, but the benefits of disrupting your opponent's rhythm with a hard service at the body are high – Jansher Khan is a past master of this technique.

You may try to practise serving with your backhand. For a right-hander, serving from the right-hand box, the backhand service means that you do not have to turn your back on your opponent.

Points to remember on the serve

(i)   The service is the only time in the rally that you have complete control of the ball, in your hand. **Don't waste it!**
(ii)   Take your time, pick your spot, and stroke right through the ball.
(iii) Step into the ball and move quickly to the 'T'.
(iv)   Develop a routine on your service which you can rely on when under pressure.
(v)   Find your opponent's weak points. Serve to your opponent's weaker side first of all. It is usually the backhand, but be aware of other flaws. If he or she is weak in the air for example, aim your service high and deep. Your target area increases against a player who is not keen on taking it early.
(vi)   Vary your service if your opponent is coping with your regular serve.
(vii) Watch your opponent. See where he or she is standing – if a player is hanging back, it probably indicates a lack of confidence in the air.

The Barrington service

Many players at the highest level use the service simply to put the ball into play. They know that a high deep service is almost certain to come back anyway, and the risk of hitting it out of court is considered too great. The notable exception to this philosophy is Britain's best player, six times British Open Champion Jonah Barrington, who uses a lob service to devastating effect.

A left hander, he serves from the left hand box with his left foot almost on the 'T'. The ball is struck high on the front wall, about two feet below the Out of Court line. It curves gently across to strike the side wall just beyond the service box, a foot inside the Out of Court line.

It has to be volleyed or it will die in the back, but to enhance the psychological effect the Great Man leaps to a crouching position on the 'T' long before the ball condescends to drop from the lights. The receiver knows that his return must be inch perfect or Jonah will be there to punish it.

By his own admission, Jonah was not the most talented player of his generation, but by honing his techniques to perfection was able to dominate world squash for a decade.

The service and service return are critical areas of the game and by refining your techniques here, you can start every rally in a dominant position.

Receiving service

The service is important for starting the rally in the right way. But receiving service is even more important. If you cannot get the service back, the rally is over. If you consistently cannot get it back, it is unlikely that you will get many chances to impress your opponent with your own service!

The ready position for receiving service (forehand left, backhand right). The racket head is up to cover your first choice of return, the volley

The ideal return of service is a ball down the side wall to a good length which takes the server back into the corner.

- Prepare for a return of serve by standing in the right place:

- Far enough away from the side wall to be able to step into the shot.

- About one foot diagonally behind the service box;

- Feet slightly angled towards the side, so that you are ready to step into the shot, but not so committed that you are unable to cover the service down the middle of the court.

- Racket head up, slightly crouched, ready for action.

Shot selection

A return of service can be to any one of four corners, and take a number of different routes and speeds to get there. Your first choice however, should be a volley back down the side wall to a length. Not every time, but it should always be there as a first option.

Your options are, in order of priority:

- Volley, before the ball reaches the side wall.

- Volley, after the ball has reached the side wall – a more difficult shot.

- Straight drive, to a length, before the ball reaches the back.

- Straight drive, off the back wall.

- A boast out of the corner.

In addition you may have the opportunity, off a weaker service, to go for straight or cross court volley kill.

The service may be returned cross court as well, either as a drive, volley, or lob, but make sure you get the width, or you will put the server in control on the 'T'.

Points to remember on returning service

(i) Keep your racket head up.

(ii) Watch your opponent, and the ball all the way.

(iii) Wait for the ball in a partial forehand or backhand posture. Not too committed, but ready to step into the shot.

(iv) Check that you are not to close to the side wall, or too far back.

(v) Remember that your first choice shot is a volley back down the side wall.

(vi) Take the ball as early as possible.

Exercises for further practice

By yourself

• • 1) To practise return of service you really need a partner or feeder. If you don't have one, then practise volleying down the side wall to yourself (see next chapter for more details).

• • 2) Throw the ball into the corner and see if you can drive it back down the side wall, rather than boast it.

With a partner

• • 3) One player serves, one returns it back down the side wall. Take ten serves each, the server scoring two points for each winning service; or one point if the service is not volleyed. The receiver scores two points for every return that reaches the back quarter of the court (Target area B, page 22), one point for a return that is good, but not in the target area. Change every ten serves, on both sides of the court.

Your personal assessment

Exercise		Day 1	Day 2	Day 3	Day 4	Day 5	Day 6	Day 7
Service*	Left box	/40	/40	/40	/40	/40	/40	/40
Service	Right box	/40	/40	/40	/40	/40	/40	/40
Serve & Return**	Left box	/40	/40	/40	/40	/40	/40	/40
	Right box	/40	/40	/40	/40	/40	/40	/40

*Each serve must hit the opposite side wall beyond the short line to score one point. Score two points if it hits the wall behind the service box and bounces before the back wall. 20 serves with a maximum score of 40.
**10 serves and returns from each side. Server scores 2 points for every winning service, 1 point for every service that is not volleyed. Receiver scores two points for every return into the back quarter of the court (Target area B, page 22). One point for every other good return. Change every ten services, do both sides of the court.

TAKING THE BALL EARLY –
THE VOLLEY

With your basic drives now working well, and a good service to start the rally, you now need to learn how to volley the ball, in other words, how to take a shot without letting it bounce.

Why volley?

One of the main objects of squash is to dominate your opponent. You cannot dominate if you are at the back of the court, scurrying around the back corners. So rather than let the ball bounce, take it on the volley, and keep your opponent behind you.

By volleying, you give your opponent less time to recover to the middle of the court from his previous shot, and thus less time to get ready for his next shot.

You can play all the shots on the volley that you can by letting it bounce, and more. You can also be more effective with the same shots because there are more angles open to you and your opponent is probably behind you, which will make your shots more effective.

Your opponent also has less time to recover between shots, and will therefore be under more pressure and more likely to get tired quickly.

By taking it early you are probably saving yourself a more difficult shot out of the back corner as well.

If you think how often the ball is in the air during a rally, it is easy to appreciate that the volley is perhaps the most important stroke in the game.

Playing an opponent who doesn't volley gives a feeling of security. He or she is not going to get in front of you, and cannot exert as much pressure and can cause less damage from the back of the court. Playing without a volley is like going fishing without a hook. By volleying you create openings, exposing cracks and flaws in your opponent's game.

How to volley

The basic straight length volley is similar to the drive in technique, but has to be modified because the ball is arriving more quickly. It is a slightly punchier shot, with less backswing.

Let us start the volley by returning to the ball control exercises on page 12.

Start one metre from the front wall only, and keep a rally going without
letting the ball bounce for as long as possible. Your wrist must be firm or

else it will be very difficult to control the ball. The swing cannot be too loose and floppy or else you will not be able to prepare for the next shot in time.

Because there is less time to prepare for the shot on a volley, it is played with less backswing than a drive, and with less follow-through. The power comes more from the wrist and forearm, rather than the whole arm or shoulder, unless you have enough time to prepare.

A firm wrist and gentle push will enable you to control the ball on the volley on this exercise, one metre from the front wall

A floppy wrist or loose swing will result in a loss of control, and you will be unable to prepare for the next shot in time

Now take the shot from two metres from the front wall. Keep your wrist firm and the swing tight and see if you can do at least ten shots without a bounce, forehand and backhand. This should be repeated all the way back to the short line.

Sometimes the ball has to be struck uncomfortably high to prevent it from going into the back corners – on the return of a lob service, for example. The temptation here is to lean back. Instead, try to take the racket back along the same line as you would for a lower volley, and attack the ball, as in the photos that follow.

You can generate neither power nor control if you lean back or let the high volley get on top of you

1 ▲

2 ▲

3 ▼

In photo 1 the striker creates space for himself by moving out of the line of the ball. Note how the elbow stays back and low (compared with the previous photo). If the elbow is too high, it presents another obstacle for the forearm and racket to overcome. By staying low, and drawing it back, there is the same smooth leverage which comes more naturally on the drive. In photos 2 and 3 the striker, having wound up for the shot, merely has to 'uncoil' the arm and racket to generate power. Note how just before and after the point of impact, the cocked wrist and open racket face mean that the racket head has travelled much further than the striker's arm. That means that it is travelling much faster, thus giving the shot power for minimum effort.

Variations on the volley

All the options available to the striker by letting the ball bounce are available on the volley, as well as some extra options. Here are six of them:

1 Volley drive

The volley drive is played with a shorter, sharper swing than the normal drive. Aim for a slightly shorter length, though, so that the ball dies as it reaches the back wall. That adds to the pressure on an opponent who is struggling to recover from the previous shot, and for whom the bounce off the back wall might otherwise offer a breathing space.

2 Volley boast

A three wall volley boast is a risky shot, because it is struck at a higher point and will therefore bounce more. The boast should not really be tried if the ball is too high, and if it is, go for a two wall boast that will die before it reaches the front wall.

3 Volley drop

The problem here is taking the speed off the ball, and there are two solutions. The first is to take no backswing and block or touch the ball into the front corner. This is best played off a hard shot which you are not able to get out of the way of in time to take a full stroke. Use the pace that your opponent has given to your own advantage.

Volley drop without backlift and follow-through

PATH OF
RACKET

The second method is to strike the ball with a lot of cut, bringing the racket down through the line of the ball to take speed off it, as shown.

Volley drop with cut

4 Volley lob

Like the standard lob in chapter 6, the volley lob is played with a short
upward push, through the ball. The principle is the same, the swing is
slightly shorter, and the touch has to be slightly more delicate off a faster
moving ball.

5 Volley kill

The loose shot within reach of the 'T' can be punished more ruthlessly on the volley than by letting it bounce. Your opponent has less time to get ready for your shot, and the height opens up a wider target angle to aim for. Make sure you make enough room for yourself to play the shot – it has to be played with you stepping in with confidence.

When most people get tired, they hang further back, behind the 'T' and volley less. When former British Closed Champion and England captain Peter Verow gets tired, he volleys more. He stays glued to the 'T' and runs less for the ball. This forces his opponent to play continually tighter shots because a player with a good reach can play most balls within reach of the 'T'. What is more difficult is having the confidence to do so the way Peter does.

Coaching tip – stamp your foot! (put your foot down!)

An attacking shot must be played with your weight going into the shot.

Some players actually stamp their foot when they step in to play an attacking shot, which acts as a check that tells you that you are balanced. Many top players have used this, notably the Australian Ken Hiscoe, and also Geoff Hunt for a time.

As a long-term solution this is not to be recommended because it may cause damage to your ankle, knee, and even hip but it does ensure that your weight is going into the shot and it helps your timing. As you step, take a pause of possibly half a second with your racket at the top of the backswing. Then the downswing.

Points to remember on the volley

(i) Keep your racket up and your wrist cocked at all times, so that you are able to take advantage of a snap volley situation.
(ii) Create as much space for yourself as possible to help you attack the ball.
(iii) Whenever you get the opportunity to volley, do so. When you have the choice of volleying or waiting, the volley is the right option to choose almost every time.
(iv) Where time allows, bring your feet around to face the side wall. When there is not enough time, at least try to get your shoulders around to the side.
(v) Play the ball away from your opponent.

Exercises for further practice

By yourself

- 1) Start close to the front wall and see how long you can keep the rally going (see top photo, page 35). See if you can do ten, and if so, try again, being aware of what the shot would look like to an outsider. Now try the backhand.

- 2) Try the same, two metres from the front wall, being forehand and backhand again.

3) Same again, one metre in front of the short line, with forehand and backhand.

4) Same again, from the short line or behind.

5) Now try hitting the ball alternately on backhand and forehand as shown below.

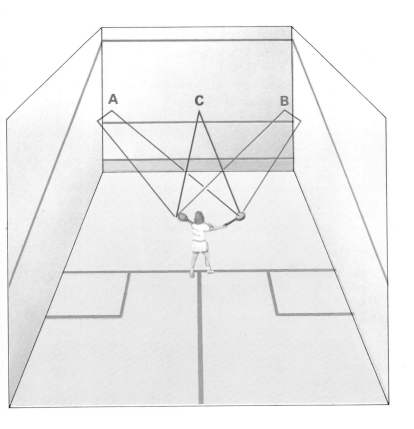

6) The same as 4, but this time keep the ball between the side of the service box and the side wall. Forehand and backhand. Try for ten.

7) Starting from the service box, and hitting close to the side wall, move one step closer to the side wall on every stroke, until you are one metre from the front wall, then move a step back on every stroke until you are behind the service box. Forehand and backhand.

8) The 'Figure of Eight' exercise as described on page 23. This is the same exercise, but now strike everything on the volley. See how long you can keep the rally going. Although this is a difficult exercise to start, it is excellent, when you can keep a rally going, for improving your shot, your timing and your concentration. Try to keep the ball at a constant height – for example, you may find that you are hitting up on the backhand and smashing more on the forehand. Try to smooth the stroke out so that it is consistent on both sides.

When this has been mastered, there are several variations:

9) As with 8, but keep the ball high, so that you are volleying everything at head height or above.

10) As with 8, but aim high on one side and volley kill to the other. Unless you continually hit dead nicks, it should be possible to keep setting the ball up for the kill. Make sure you practise equally on forehand and backhand.

11) As with 8, but now bring the front wall directly ahead of the 'T' into play as well (position C in the diagram on page 26). This can be done with various combinations of the three positions, e.g. set the ball up in position C and either volley drive or kill the ball to position A or B.

With a partner

12) Starting with both players on the short line, hit the ball back to each other, seeing how long you can keep the ball going without a bounce. Aim for twenty on both forehand and backhand.

13) Starting from the back of the service box, Player A hits a high volley back down the side wall to him- or herself and then crosscourts a similar high lob volley. On the other side of the court, player B does likewise, and the rally continues for as long as possible without a bounce. Try to make every shot, straight or cross court, as tight as possible, rather than simply feeding yourself.

14) Exercise 12 can be made into a game, where players score a point if they can get the ball to bounce in the opposite back quarter of the court.

15) Play a normal game, but with the additional rule that the ball is not allowed to touch the back wall. If player A plays a drive or volley which player B is unable to intercept before the back wall, a point goes to player A. The only other proviso is that the ball is not allowed to hit the back wall without a bounce. If player A overhits the ball so that it hits the back without bouncing, a point goes to player B.

Your personal assessment

Exercise	Forehand/Backhand	Day 1	Day 2	Day 3	Day 4	Day 5	Day 6	Day 7
1	FH							
	BH							
2	FH							
	BH							
3	FH							
	BH							
4	FH							
	BH							
5 *1								
6	FH							
	BH							
7 *1	FH							
	BH							
8 *1								
9 *1								

*1 Aim for ten shots; then twenty; then thirty; keep pushing back the barriers of physical and mental tiredness!

USING THE SIDE WALLS – BOASTS AND ANGLES

One of the pleasures of squash is the variety of shots and options which the side and back walls can add. A shot played off the side wall is called a boast, or angle.

In this section we will look at the boast, how and when to play it and then consider variations on the shot. At the end of the section you will again find a personal assessment sheet on which to gauge your improvement.

The boast is a two-edged sword. It opens up a whole range of defensive and attacking possibilities. It also opens up the court for your opponent, and if played badly, or played at the wrong time, it can get you into more trouble than it's worth.

How to play a boast

The classic three wall boast is played from the back of the court, off the side wall, to finish as close as possible to the nick in the opposite front corner.

The technique is similar to a drive. It does not have to be hit exceptionally hard, but it does need to be high enough to carry to the front wall; and the angle has to be good enough to finish close to the nick. A badly hit boast will invariably 'sit up' for your opponent or come back to the middle of the court.

The diagram opposite gives an idea of the angle at which to strike a boast.

Point A is the point of impact. If the ball is hit too deeply into the side (Path C, Green), it will not reach the front. Path D (yellow) shows the ball which is hit too straight and narrow. The angle is not enough to carry the ball to the front corner and it will come back within easy reach of your opponent on the 'T'. But the ball which is hit down path B (red) strikes the front wall about a metre from the opposite corner and either catches the nick, or the side wall just above the nick.

The stance for a boast is thus similar to that for a drive, but with the position of address 45 degrees around towards the back corners as shown in the second diagram.

The red footprints and point of impact 'A' show the path of a drive while the green footprints and point of impact 'B' show the comparative stance for a boast.

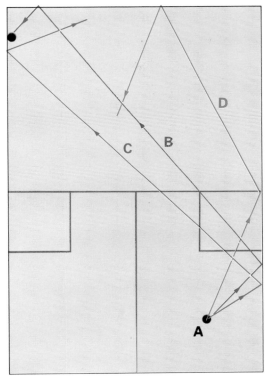

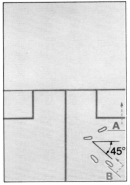

To practise the shot by yourself, set the ball up against the side wall, at the back of the service box, and strike the ball at about 45 degrees to the side, to finish up in the opposite corner. It may take a lot of practice to get the angle correctly.

Coaching tip – how to angle the boast

Many people struggle to get the correct angle on the ball when they learn to play the boast. It comes naturally to some (people who have played snooker, for example) but others may struggle.

If you struggle, try any of these three tips:

1) Try to imagine that the side wall you are facing is not there. Instead, you can see straight through to the next court. Picture the opposite front corner of the next court, and imagine that you are going to play a straight drive towards it. That will give you the correct angle.

2) Alternatively, picture the side wall as a mirror, in which you can see the opposite front corner, and aim towards it.

3) If that doesn't work, try putting a straight object, such as a spare racket on a line at 45 degrees to the side wall. Try playing a straight drive down the line of the racket. If the angle is not right, then adjust the direction of the racket accordingly.

When do I boast?

The first use for the boast is **defence**, to get the ball out of a back corner. Because of the back wall, you may not be able to take a full swing to drive the ball out, but if you exaggerate your stance and turn to face the back corner, you can take a full swing, with the racket coming down parallel to the back wall. As you get better at it, and build up confidence, so you can get closer and closer to the back corner.

Watch the top players, and you will see the ball coming back from within inches of the back wall.

Secondly, the boast can be used for **attack**, from either the back or front of the court. If you sense your opponent is beginning to tire and hang behind the 'T', a well played boast interspersed with the drives will make it even harder for him.

Thirdly, it is a **working** shot, moving your opponent around the court, dragging him to the front before you push him all the way back again.

Squash is a game of angles which is what distinguishes it from most other racket sports and gives the game variety; make the most of them.

Improving your boast

There are three important points which may help you improve the way you play a boast:
1) Don't crowd the ball. Most beginners get too close to the back or side wall when they try to play the boast. You must have enough room to swing the racket without cramping the swing because you are too close.

Here the striker has enough room to play a good boast. If his feet were any closer to the back wall or the side wall, he would not have room to swing the racket properly. The feet must not simply move towards the wall, they must move to a position where you can take a full balanced swing at the ball.

2) Don't force the shot. To get maximum turn from the racket, which is vital if you are to get the more difficult balls out, you need the racket to turn in as tight an area as possible. That means allowing the racket to swing past you. If you physically try to help the ball on its way, you will end up taking more space, and getting less turn on the racket head.

49

In the photo above the racket is whipping through and past the arm. That means that the racket head is turning in a very tight area. If you physically force the shot, the arm is moving more, and therefore the racket head has to travel further to turn, thus wasting valuable space in the back corner. Good backhand technique below left, and bad, right

3) Don't be frightened to turn right around to the back wall to get the ball out. Tennis and badminton players in particular are used to playing the ball in front of them, and at worst, beside them, and often have trouble letting a ball go past their body. To get the right angle, however, a boast must be struck when the ball *has* gone behind you.

Variations on the boast

So far we have concentrated on the three wall boast, hit to finish in the opposite nick, but there are a multitude of variations.

The best lesson I had on the boast came from a mentor, Zimbabwean Barry Bakewell who, musing over his staple diet of a glass of water and a banana said: 'You know, I could write a book about the boast. I think I will one day'.

To the best of my knowledge it is still in the pipeline, but, although he didn't expand on this revelation, he did something better.

He left me wondering what he could have meant. Until that point I had thought of the boast as a shot played simply to get out of trouble in the back corners, and occasionally as an attacking surprise shot.

Barry left me to work all the possible permutations out for myself – the different angles, speeds and heights that the ball could be played at, the times when it could be used which I had not previously considered and the positions on court that it can be played from.

He was right: you could write a book on the boast – but it is better to work it out for yourself!

Here are a few variations, but for the best results, do as I did and work out variations for yourself. Try them out in practice sessions. See if they work and how they can be used to best effect.

Don't get disheartened if they don't come off first of all. The deceptive shots which you see at the top in most sports are rarely as spontaneous as they look, and come about as a result of a lot of sweat on the practice court!

1 The trickle boast

Hit softly as an alternative to either the drive or drop shot, the trickle boast is played at the front of the court by bringing the arm through the shot before the racket, so that the racket is 'left behind' and angles into the side wall. The trickle boast is played with your body in a similar position to that in which you would strike a drive or drop. Only the racket angle, and possibly the point of impact, should change.

2 The two wall boast

Robert Owen, ranked in the world's top twenty, is a master of the two wall boast, which dies before it reaches the side wall. The advantages are that it dies quickly and that it is travelling across the opponent's line as he or she steps towards it – it is therefore harder to hit. The disadvantage is that it is a riskier shot than the standard boast. It needs to be played at a slightly narrower angle than the standard boast, but it must also be hit closer to the tin, so that it does not reach the side wall. It needs to be hit with 'cut' to make it die quickly off the front wall. At over six feet tall, Robert is able to come down on the ball, playing it closer to his body than for a normal boast, and thereby adding the necessary spin.

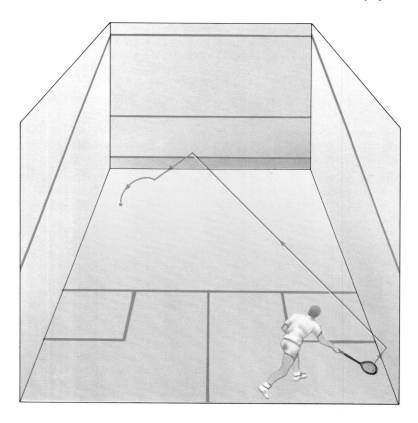

3 The lob boast

Played from the back corner, this shot basically buys time, enabling you to recover to the 'T' before your opponent can play the next shot. A risky shot, it must be hit higher and softer than a normal three wall boast, dipping down into the front corner (see below, blue path).

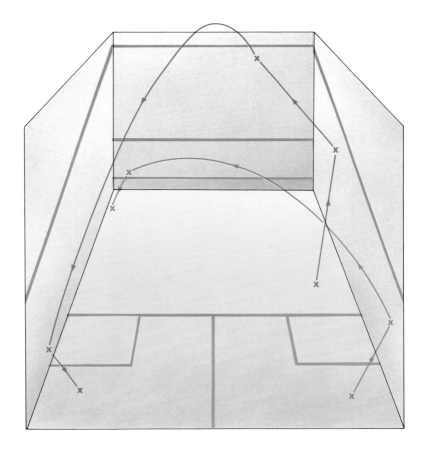

4 The skid boast

Played high and hard off the side wall, with a much narrower trajectory than a standard boast, it is aimed to finish in the opposite back corner. Over the last few years, this has become more of a standard shot in the leading players' repertoire (see above, green path).

5 The reverse angle

Played to the opposite side wall to the conventional boast, the reverse angle requires a little more space than usual and is used to wrong-foot an opponent. It is a particularly effective reply to a loose service, loose drop or a drive lacking length and width. (See below.)

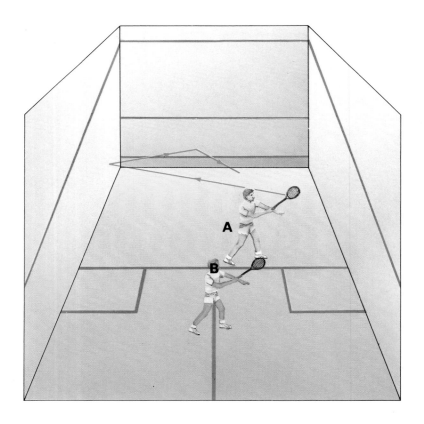

Player B has played a weak shot to the middle of the court, and Player A now has a wide range of options, of which the reverse angle is an effective but occasional choice. The dangers are that, if played badly, the ball will come straight back at you. In the interests of safety, it should not be played from the back of the court

Exercises for further practice

By yourself

- 1) Throw the ball off the side wall and practise the angle and trajectory of the boast. This can be varied by throwing off the back wall, and by throwing from the back wall to come off the side or onto the side wall to come off the back. If you have trouble getting the ball out, start from nearer the front wall.

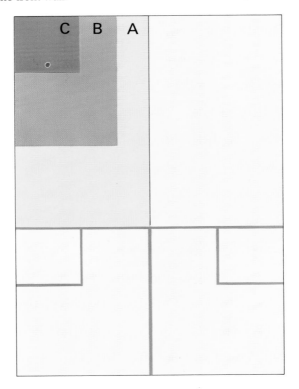

A, B and C represent target areas for the boast. Target A is for beginners and represents ¼ of the court. Target B is more difficult and can be drawn on the court with the chalk, or using plastic tape. The more advanced target C is the size of the service box

- 2) Play straight drives and intersperse every third or fourth shot with a boast, then continue with drives on the other side wall for three or four shots.

With a partner

- 3) Player A hits cross court to hit the side wall and bounce behind the service box. Player B boasts. Do this on both sides. (See below.)

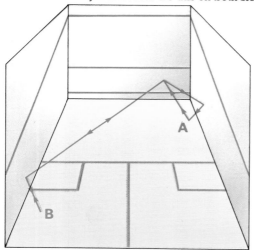

- • 4) Player A drives a straight forehand. Player B boasts on the forehand. Player A drives a straight backhand. Player B boasts on the backhand. The rally continues. (See below.)

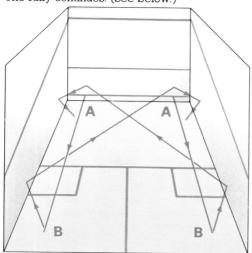

- 5) Player A drives straight, B boasts, A plays a drop shot, B drives straight, A boasts, B plays a drop shot, and so on.

Your personal assessment

Assess your progress with these exercises on the chart below:

Exercise	Forehand/ Backhand	Day 1	Day 2	Day 3	Day 4	Day 5	Day 6	Day 7
1 Target A	FH							
	BH							
1 Target B	FH							
	BH							
1 Target C	FH							
	BH							
3 Target A *1	FH							
	BH							
3 Target B	FH							
	BH							
3 Target C	FH							
	BH							
4 Target A *1								
4 Target B								
4 Target C								
5 *2								

*1 How many shots in succession can you get into the target area in the course of a rally?
*2 How many shots can you keep the rally going for with your partner?

● ● 6) Play a normal game except that both players have the option of playing only a straight drive or a boast.

There are many variations on these exercises but the above cover the primary movements.

Exercises 3 and 4 require fairly advanced movement and ball control skills – don't be disheartened if you find it difficult to start with, because you will improve quickly and they are commonly used by top players as well as beginners.

Exercise 5 is more difficult still, but does instil good habits – the best shot to play off a boast is a straight drop shot (see Saturday, page 00), while a length drive is the best option off a drop. A boast may be the only option, when replying to a good drive.

Exercise 6 is a tactical game which requires not only control of the drive and boast, but will also help you to develop perception of when to play it and deception in its execution. Although you are limited to playing only two shots, they finish up in diagonally opposite corners of the court and so can be very tiring as well!

Points to remember on the boast

(i)   Don't play it too often – as a defensive shot, your first choice should be a drive or a volley. As an attacking shot, a weak boast will give your opponent control of the front of the court.
(ii) Make sure you have enough room to play the shot.
(iii) If you cannot get enough width on your shot, turn further towards the back corner.
(iv) Keep the swing tight in the back corners.

THE TOUCH GAME – DROPS AND LOBS

The drop shot

A squash court is a large room with four awkward corners. Forcing your opponent to spend a lot of time in these corners is one of the pleasures of the game!

Today's lesson will concentrate on the two most important 'touch' shots in squash: the **drop** and the **lob**. Both shots are played to stretch your opponent into positions he would rather not go: these are low and high into the front and back corners.

Like any object, the squash court has three physical dimensions: length, width and height. Because a squash court is longer than it is wide, the most difficult movements are forwards and backwards. While drives and lobs take the ball to the back corners, the drop is the most direct route to the front.

Where to play a drop. The perfect drop should hit the front wall a few inches above the tin, dropping into the side wall nick, giving your opponent little chance even if he reads it correctly (path A). The ball on path B hits the front and then the side wall before the floor. The side wall takes speed off the ball and ensures that your opponent will have to stretch well forward. The ball on path C hits the front wall, then the floor, before reaching the side. This shot should be hit to reach the side wall on the second bounce, thus making it a difficult shot to retrieve.

How to play the drop shot

Preparation for the drop is similar to that for a drive. The position of address and the point of impact are similar, but the execution is different.

These are the most important points to remember when playing the drop:

(i) Take the racket back to shoulder height – far enough back to play a drive as necessary, but not so far back that you cannot control the downswing for the softer drop shot.

Preparation for the drop shot. The swing is not shorter, but the racket face is open so that the striker keeps all the options open

Compare this with the preparation for a drive which has a longer backswing and a more powerful downswing

(ii) Keep your grip light. This helps you to 'feel' the racket head in the same way that you would hold a pen to write. Clutch it too tightly and you will not feel the position of the racket head and you will struggle to move it. Try holding your pen too tightly and notice the loss of control in your writing.

(iii) Keep the racket face open as you bring the racket down. With a drive, the racket head will whip through the ball.

With a drop shot, the racket and arm move more in unison. The open racket face keeps your options open to play a drive, boast or cross court shot, with a similar stance and taking the ball within the 'impact zone'.

The open racket race helps you to develop 'cut' on the ball. The racket does not hit the ball square on, but at an angle. This causes the ball to spin and to spend longer on the strings, thus cutting down its speed.

When first trying this shot for the first time, only put a little 'cut' on the ball, and bring the shot into your repertoire only as and when you feel that you can control it.

At the point of impact, your racket and arm should be stroking through the ball together with your racket face open to help cut the ball. The dotted line shows how the racket is totally under control throughout the 'impact zone', which gives the shot greater stability.

(iv) Bend your knees. Get down to the level of the ball – not only does that give you better reach, but it also puts you in a more dynamic position to control the shot *and* to spring back to the 'T' at he end of it.

(v) Make sure that you hit 'through' the ball, not at it (bottom left hand photo). The racket is moving at the same speed and angle before, during and after the point of impact. Aim for consistency throughout the whole of the impact zone. That gives you greater control of the ball's speed and direction than is possible with a more 'wristy' shot.

An analogy would be to compare the impact zone with shooting. A man with a pistol cannot control a bullet over long distances the way a man with a rifle can. The longer barrel on a rifle gives far greater control over distance, time and space for the barrel to 'fine tune' the path of the bullet. That is what the impact zone does to the ball – it fine tunes the path of the ball for greater accuracy and consistency.

One of the most common faults on the drop shot is the temptation to hit **at** the ball, rather than **through** it. This leads to a 'stabbing' action which gives considerably less control over the ball. The cure is to concentrate on hitting through the ball, keeping your mind not on the point of impact, but on how the racket will finish up. Keep your head steady throughout the shot for control.

(vi) Step into the shot. The drop cannot be played effectively if you are off balance or, more specifically, leaning backwards. It is hard to keep your touch if half your mind is concentrated on keeping you upright!

When to play the drop shot

The general rule for playing drops is very simple: if your opponent is in front of you, play the ball to the back of the court, but if your opponent is behind you, the drop shot should be a first choice option. You can see the reason for this in the two right hand photos:

Player B is now striking the drop shot. This time the ball has further to go to reach the front wall and will take longer to get there. Player B's target is smaller because he is farther away. Player A does not have too far to go to get the shot, and he doesn't have to negotiate his opponent's body to get there either!

Another general rule is to play more length shots at the beginning of the match, and keep your drops to a minimum. As your opponent starts to hang back, or get tired, you can start to introduce the drops. Don't play too many drops too early in the match or you will simply give your opponent control of the front of the court.

Player A is well placed to play a straight drop shot. The ball will not take long to reach the front wall, the target area is close and Player B has a long way to go to reach the ball. In addition, he has the problem of getting round Player A Now consider the opposite scenario. Player B is now playing a drop shot. He is a long way from the front so the ball has further to travel. His opponent is in front of him and well placed to pick up a drop shot.

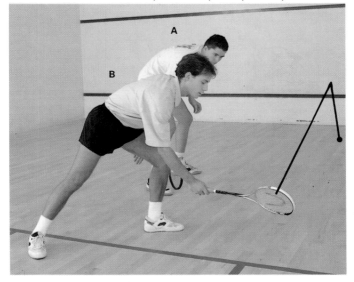

Coaching tip – address the ball the way a bullfighter would!

The drop is often played in reply to a weak shot around the middle of the court. Getting into position to play a ball coming towards you is just as important as your position when chasing the ball.

Try to copy the techniques of the bullfighter when faced with a charging bull. Very few bullfighters make it to the top by standing behind their red cape, for obvious reasons!

Few squash players make it to the top who do not make room to play their shot.

A bullfighter moves to side-step his adversary, moving his cape to the side to allow the bull to pass. When the ball approaches you, side-step it in the same way, so that your racket has room to swing and, therefore, more control over the ball you are playing.

Similarly, when running to the front of the court, leave enough room between yourself and the side wall to allow the ball to pass down the corridor you have left without obstruction. Get too close and you not only play a bad shot, but you get in the way of it on its path back as well!

Exercises for further practice

By yourself

When practising the drop shot by yourself, use a red or blue dot squash ball. The extra bounce will make practice a lot easier.

- 1) Set the ball up for yourself by throwing it off the front wall, so that it bounces back about two to three metres from the front and one metre from the side. Your shot should be hit below the cut line, and strike the side wall before the floor. Start well away from the side wall so that you give yourself a large target area and gradually move nearer to the side. Practise both backhand and forehand.

- 2) Now try a continuous sequence hitting one drop shot, and then pushing the ball back further thus setting up another drop. By way of variation try a continuous drop sequence to improve your touch. Again, practise backhand and forehand.

- 3) Set up a target area (see right, yellow area) and see how many shots you can do from strike position A. See if you can do ten consecutive shots on both backhand and forehand.

- 4) Now aim for the green area, ten consecutive shots again, backhand and forehand.

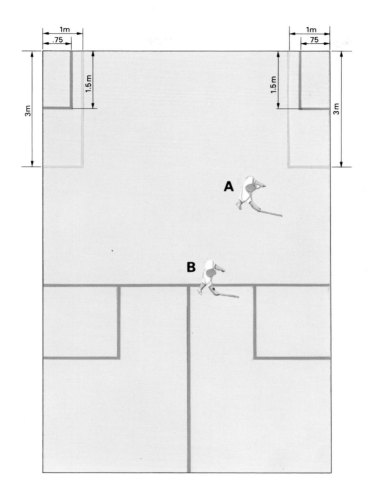

- 5) Move back to hitting position B on the short line and try for ten consecutive shots into the green target area.

- 6) Play a high angled shot across the court and then a straight drop. Boast the drop again and play another straight drop. As you get into it, keep the boast lower. This exercise gets more strenuous the better you get at it! See how long you can keep the rally going without hitting the ball above the cut line at all.

With a partner

- 7) Player A feeds Player B. Make sure you get back to the 'T' between shots. Start with easy feeds and make it more difficult as you get better, to see if you can keep up the same quality of shot under pressure.

- 8) Player A plays a boast, Player B drops, A straight drives, B boasts, A drops, B drives. Keep a continuous rally going (not trying to beat each other!) for as long as possible. To make it more competitive, play ten shots like this and then both players try to win the rally, keeping the same shot routine with shots that must be within the target areas.

- 9) Player A drives, Player B boasts, A drops, B drops, A drives, B boasts, and so on. As with exercise 8 keep a co-operative rally going, and to make it more competitive, try to win the rally after the tenth shot.

- 10) Play a normal game but play that every boast must be followed by a drop shot.

- 11) Another game. After the service, every shot must be played to bounce in front of the short line.

Points to remember on the drop shot

The drop is a very rewarding shot when played well – if you play badly, you will pay a high price. To make sure that you play it well, remember these points:

(i)   Only play a drop when you are in front of your opponent.

(ii)   Prepare your racket at shoulder height, with your wrist firm and fingers relaxed.

(iii) Check your position of address. Don't get too close – remember the bullfighter.

(iv)   Hit through the ball, not at it.

(v)   Keep the racket face open for cut and control.

(vi)   Keep the racket head steady and open as it passes through the 'impact zone'.

(vii) The drop shot should never come back further than the striker. If it does, he or she is left completely exposed.

The lob

Of the three dimensions of a squash court (length, width and height), the most neglected is **height**. Many squash players are preoccupied with hitting the ball hard. They have the importance of length and width drummed in to them quite rightly, but then ignore the third dimension: height.

Your personal assessment

Exercise	Forehand/Backhand	Day 1	Day 2	Day 3	Day 4	Day 5	Day 6	Day 7
3	FH							
	BH							
4	FH							
	BH							
5	FH							
	BH							
6*								

*Record your longest rally.

The lob can be both a key defensive and attacking shot. As a defensive shot, the lob buys you time to recover when your opponent has stranded you away from the centre of the court. It can be used to slow the game down when you are under pressure or feeling tired. As an attacking shot, it can be used to break down the resistance of a poor volleyer. And a good length lob will die as surely in the back corner as a hard hit drive!

How to play the lob

As with the drop shot, the lob is a 'touch' shot. To keep control of your racket, while at the same time maintaining the delicate feel for the shot, keep your wrist firm, your fingers relaxed, and an open face on your racket.

A lob must be hit to a good **length**, so that it reaches the back of the court but does not come off the back wall. It must be hit to a good **width**, so that it doesn't go out on the side wall, or come back too close to the centre. Most importantly, it must have **height** – it must be high enough to pass your opponent's outstretched racked, or else it presents him or her with a very easy shot.

To get that height you must exaggerate three points of basic technique – take the ball well in front of the front foot, keep the face of your racket open and get right down to the level of the ball (by bending your knees), so that you can get under it with your racket.

Note the differences in technique between the lob (right) and the drive (left). The striker's knees are well bent on the lob, allowing him to get right down to the level of the ball. That gives more control, allowing the racket to get below the ball, before rising and lifting it to the back of the court. As a lob is often played under pressure from the front of the court, you are naturally stretching and in the best position to play what is tactically a very good shot

The ball is struck well in front of the front foot in the lob. That means that the racket is naturally starting to rise, making a lob the natural shot. It would be hard to 'manufacture' the height necessary to play a lob if the point of impact was the same as in the drive.

One side effect of this is that a cross court shot is also more naturally played when the ball is well in front of you. A cross court lob (see diagram below, path A) is thus often the natural choice under pressure, rather than the straight lob (see diagram below, path B).

A good length cross court lob should loop to the back of the court, hitting the side wall just short of the back wall.

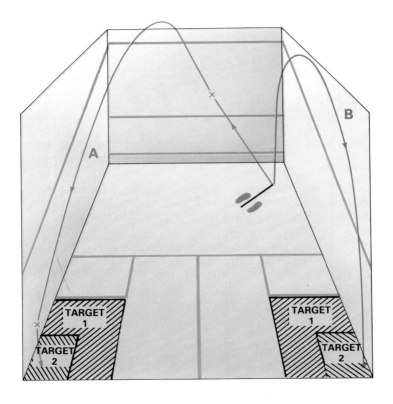

Target areas for the lob. Whether straight or cross court, the lob is hit deeper than the drive because it will not bounce off the back wall to the same extent, and because a short lob will expose the striker more than a short drive

Exercises for further practice

By yourself

- 1) Starting from the short line, set the ball up and see if you can lob it over your own head. Make sure you are able to get both height and length on the shot. If not, aim higher on the front wall. If you still cannot get the height, ghost the shot, watch your swing as you do it and check that you are coming right underneath the ball. Try to hit ten shots out of ten over your outstretched racket so that they finish behind the service box. (Target area, illustrated on page 69). Do this for the forehand and backhand sides.

- 2) Now try boasting the ball gently from the short line and lob it straight to the back of the court. Try for ten into the target area on both (see page 69) forehand and backhand.

- 3) The same as exercise 2, but using the cross court lob.

With a partner

- 4) Player A plays a straight drop shot, Player B lobs straight. Try this on the forehand then on the backhand. This can either be played with A feeding B, to practise the stroke, or as a game, where each player has to keep the ball within the respective target areas for lob and drop, losing the point if he or she misses.

- 5) Player A boasts the ball, Player B lobs it straight down the side. The rally continues. See how long you can keep a rally going using the target areas, and then make it competitive, losing points for bad shots.

- 6) Player A lobs straight, B boasts, A plays a straight drop, B lobs straight, A boasts, B drops straight and so on. See if you can keep the rally going for twenty shots. Then be more competitive, by keeping the rally going for ten shots and then trying to win it.

- • 7) Play a normal game, but neither player is allowed to hit the ball hard.

Points to remember on the lob

(i)   Aim high on the front wall. If you are not reaching the back, aim to hit higher, not harder.

(ii) Keep your racket face open throughout the shot.

(iii) Bend your knees.

(iv) Strike the ball well in front of you.

(v)   Keep a high follow-through for control and 'fine tuning'.

Your personal assessment

Exercise	Forehand/ Backhand	Day 1	Day 2	Day 3	Day 4	Day 5	Day 6	Day 7
1	FH							
	BH							
2	FH							
	BH							
3	FH							
	BH							

PUTTING IT ALL TOGETHER

Now that we have the components of the game – the shots, the movements, the techniques – we have to put them together to form a coherent whole.

The shots are only tools, and to play squash successfully, they have to be played in the right place, at the right time, and as part of an overall strategy.

There are several general rules that should be followed (such as keeping the ball in the corners, trying to dominate the 'T', etc.) which apply whether you are an absolute beginner or a world champion. For example, everyone will find it more difficult to return a shot that is close to the side wall and bouncing near the back than to return an easy shot from the middle of the court.

What, then, are these rules?

Here are nine key tactics which will help you play better squash; they are the rudiments of tactical play. Don't take them as gospel, but use them as a dynamic base for your game:

1 Control the 'T'

Two simple facts about the game of squash should convince you of the importance of dominating the centre of the court, the 'T'.

Firstly, if you are on the 'T', you are within two steps of virtually anything your opponent can hit at you and secondly, if *you* are on the 'T', your opponent is not. Unlike tennis or badminton, where your opponent is safely out of the way on the other side of the net, in squash you are not only close to your opponent but you are vying for the same prized position.

So try to make sure that your shots force your opponent away from he 'T' area. The photo opposite shows the area that can be covered without leaving the 'T'. If your shots come back within reach of that area, your opponent does not have to leave his central position to return them.

The 'T' must be the base to which you return after every shot – make sure that you make every effort to get back to it. You may feel tired, but if you do not make the extra effort to cover the 'T', all your other efforts will count for nothing.

Your reach from the 'T'. The shaded area shows the amount of court that can be covered without actually leaving the 'T' area.

2 Always hit a penetrating length

A good length is the key ingredient to both attacking and defensive squash. A well hit drive will not hit the back wall directly, nor will it finish short. It should bounce in the red shaded area shown in the diagram on page 74 at the back of the court. Ideally, it will bounce once and then die in the back corner.

Similarly, a good length drop shot will bounce inside the red shaded area at the front of the court (see page 74). The green shaded areas represent a moderate length drop or drive while the unshaded area represents a poor drive or drop. A ball that lands in this area ought to be punished.

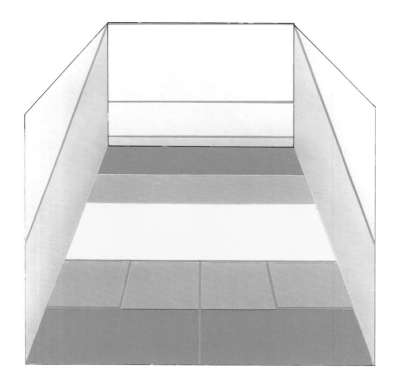

A good length

As a general rule, the ball should be hit to a good length in the back corners in preference to the front corners. The short shot is a double-edged sword, which can work against you if played too often or too early in the game by giving your opponent too many options. A weak return is certain when your opponent is well and truly buried in the back corner by a good length shot.

Don't give your opponent the front of the court for nothing – allow him or her the opportunity to go forward only when you know that he or she cannot return your shot, or when you know that you can cover his or her options.

Good length comes with practice and can be achieved by hitting hard or soft, the determining factor being the ball's trajectory on to the front wall. The decision as to whether to play hard or soft depends on the state of the game, the state of your opponent, and your general match plan. But the *length* of the shot, whatever its speed, should always be your primary consideration.

3 Keep it close to the side walls

The closer the ball is to the side wall, the harder it is to hit and the fewer your opponent's options. It stands to reason therefore that a shot down the nearside wall is generally speaking a better shot to play than a cross court one.

Beginners tend to play far too many cross courts – as a tactical rule, play the straight shot through choice and always play it straight if you are in doubt.

The general rule should be to hit the side wall at a point level with where your opponent is standing, whether you are hitting straight or crosscourt.

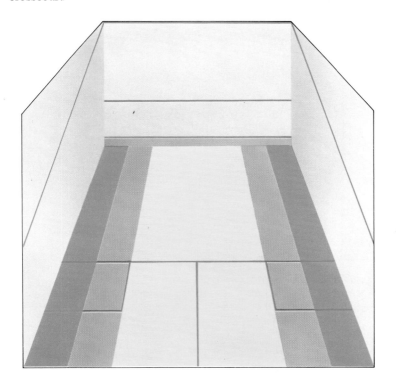

A good width shot should finish in the red shaded areas. The green shaded area is a reasonable target for the beginner, but is not penetrating enough to pressurise an opponent. The unshaded area is a definite no-go area!

When the cross court is played, it must be wide enough to get past your opponent. A good cross court will hit the side wall at the back of the service box or beyond, so that it dies in the back corner. But if your opponent is standing up on the 'T', or is good on the volley, aim wider to keep your shot out of reach, as shown below.

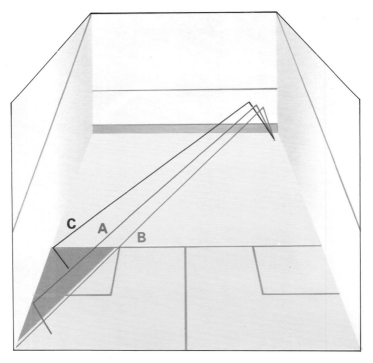

The red shaded area shows the target area for a cross court drive. The ideal standard trajectory would be path A. Path B can be penetrating if your opponent is hanging back or unwilling to volley the ball. If your opponent is standing forward, keep the ball out of reach by using Path C. The danger here is that the ball will come wide off the side wall back towards the middle, so it is unwise to use this shot if your opponent is hanging back

4 Take the ball early

The virtues of volleying the ball have been fully extolled in Chapter 4 (Thursday); nevertheless, it is necessary to recap on the tactical rule that to dominate and control the game you need to be in front of your opponent.

Why?

(i) Because you have a greater range of shots open to you than if you take the ball further back, after it has bounced.

(ii) Because your opponent has had less time to recover from his previous shot and is therefore likely to be out of position and to tire more quickly.

(iii) Because you are saving yourself a longer trip into the back corner and making your next shot easier as well.

By taking the ball earlier than your opponent, you can dominate the 'T', and hence the game. Playing an opponent who cannot volley gives you the security of knowing that he or she cannot hurt you – make sure that you are not that sort of opponent!

5 Watch the ball!

That sounds easy! The problem is that if you play a good penetrating length, the action is now going on behind you, and there is a temptation to watch the front wall and wait for the ball to come into view.

Train yourself to watch the ball off the strings of the racket. This is not as easy as it sounds, because of the speed of the racket and ball at the point of impact, but the longer you watch, the clearer the picture in your mind as to where you will need to move next.

If you are staring at the front wall, with your opponent playing the ball from behind you, there is a good chance you will find out where the ball is the hard way when it hits you!

Coaching tip – avoid the 'panic button'!

When you are under pressure and you do not know what to do next, the body has a simple response – Panic!

The body releases adrenalin which stimulates the flow of blood to the heart. That surge allows you to focus clearly on an immediate course of action, and it gives you extra strength and speed to follow that course. In its most basic form, it allows you to run faster. Properly controlled, that surge of adrenalin can lift you to unexpected heights. But it can also lead to a blinkered single-mindedness.

On a squash court the usual result of a shot of adrenalin is to make you want to chase the ball faster, rather than try to dominate the 'T'. The result is that you end up running around the court like a headless chicken and get very tired!

This is the moment when clear thought is crucial – keep it simple and stick to a simple tactical plan. For example, observe the first tactical rule on our list – dominating the 'T' – or the second – playing the ball straight rather than cross court.

By focusing on one point, you channel all your nervous energy into a constructive direction, not an aimless one!

When you feel the urge to press the mental 'panic button', take your time and use the surge of adrenalin constructively – don't simply allow your legs to do your thinking for you! You will get tired quickly, your shots will become predictable and you will lose control of the game.

6 Long from the back, short from the front

It sounds simple and it is simple. Your opponent should be made to cover the maximum distance possible, as often as possible.

When you are in front of your opponent, the court is at your mercy. You can play winners to the front and your shots to the back will be more penetrating. So when your opponent is in front of you, your primary concern must be to get him or her behind you.

If you play a short shot from the back of the court (other than as a rarely used surprise tactic), your opponent will be well placed to pick it up – he or she will have more time to reach it and a shorter distance to travel. The chances of you playing a weak shot or making a mistake are also higher.

However, a short shot when your opponent is behind you gives you a closer, easier target, the ball will take less time to reach the front, and your opponent has further to travel (and he or she has to get around you as well!).

Playing a short shot with your opponent behind you

7 Play the percentage game

Because a squash court is relatively small while the target area (the front wall) is relatively large, rallies can be very long. Rallies of one hundred shots or more are not uncommon at a high level.

Eliminating unnecessary errors should be an important tactical consideration. That does not mean that you should play negative squash, but you should make a point of cutting out the shots that you make too many mistakes on. Make sure that you have a reasonable margin for error on the shot, particularly when playing the ball short. If you aim close to the tin, you may well gain more outright winners, but you will certainly make a lot more mistakes as well. At a top class level, there are few outright winners in squash. Be aware of your areas of weakness and strive to eliminate, or improve, them in practice.

A winning shot is one that is played in the right place at the right time, and does not necessarily have to be played an inch above the tin.

Coaching tip – use the knock-up!

The knock-up is a period of five minutes at the beginning of a match which is used to warm up your body and the ball. It is also an opportunity to assess your opponent's strengths and weaknesses.

To get your own game back into the groove, start off by gently building a rhythm in your shots. The temptation is to start too quickly. If you are worried or excited at the prospect of the match ahead, the extra adrenalin will make you try too hard too quickly. By pacing yourself, you are able to establish a rhythm and build on it over the five minutes allowed. If you start too quickly, you will probably not establish as efficient a rhythm, and you will have allowed your opponent to get used to your pace.

Work to get a consistent length as well. You want to be able to slip easily into a 'grooved' length as soon as the game begins.

Watch your opponent to see if you can glean any insight into his or her game before play starts. You may be able to make some early assumptions before a ball is hit by noting things like your opponent's size and apparent physical condition.

On court, watch your opponent's swing. It may appear weaker on one side than the other. For example, he or she may hang further back on the backhand side than on the forehand – that is a sure sign of a lack of confidence.

Hit a few shots in the air, and see if your opponent is keen to volley, or to let the ball bounce? Does he or she appear to struggle in the back corners?

What about any particular shots that you will need to be ready for when the game starts?

Keep these points in mind for the game, and most importantly, get your own game going. It is *your* game that you are going to impose on your opponent, and it should be functioning smoothly before the first point is played.

8 The five dimensions of a squash court

A squash court has five dimensions – five variables that you can use to your advantage in a game if you are aware of them.

They are length, width, height, time and speed. Let's look at them each in turn:

Length

We have already discussed length, and the value of a penetrating length, in some detail. A deep length is hard to retrieve; a short length, as in a drop shot, is also very difficult to return. But hardest of all is a game that mixes the two, and pushes your opponent into the back corners and then drags him or her forward again when he or she starts to hang back. Vary your length, but keep the emphasis on the deeper shots.

Width

To get the most out of the width of a court, keep the ball close to the side walls, and go cross court occasionally, but hit the ball wide enough to ensure that your opponent has to go right back or well forward, and not just sideways, to reach it.

Height

Get the most out of the size and shape of a squash court by stretching your opponent upwards – push him into the back corners with high, deep shots and stretch him forwards with short, low ones.

Time

By taking the ball early, you deprive your opponent of time – as well as saving yourself the trouble of running to the back corners! By volleying, you apply pressure. By the same token, you can slow the game down if you are under pressure by letting the ball bounce or by hitting it straight and high down the side walls and thus 'buying' yourself time.

Speed

Speed is a weapon of variable force. You may well apply pressure by hitting the ball hard, but often you can apply just as much pressure with a soft shot. Choose the right speed for the shot in hand. Speed is a weapon, but it is one that can be blunted if it is used too often, too early. If your opponent is susceptible to speed, use it; otherwise, apply it more sparingly.

9 Keep your opponent guessing!

A good technique gives you the option of playing many different shots from the same position. By keeping your options open, you are staying one step ahead of your opponent the whole time.

With practice, you will be able to play the ball to any one of the four corners, at different heights and speeds, from almost any position on court.

In photo 1 you see a standard preparation for the forehand drive. With slight variations in the point of impact, a full range of shots is open to the striker, as shown in photos 2 and 3.

1

2

3

With sound technique, all these variations are possible with practice. Work on the basic techniques discussed in this book, and you will have a sound platform from which to launch your squash career!

FIT FOR SQUASH

This is not a book on fitness, but to get the best out of your squash, you need to be fit to play it. That means you need to supplement your practice and games on court with the right sort of exercise on- and off-court.

To reduce the risk of injury, it is important to warm your body up before you start, even if it is only for five minutes. Like starting a car on a cold morning, you can damage the 'engine' if you do too much too soon. Most muscle strains occur in the first ten minutes on court, when the player makes a sharp stretching movement after the ball before the body is properly warmed up.

It is also important to 'warm down' at the end of a match or training session. This prevents stiffness in the muscles, particularly if you have not done any exercise for a while.

Before you start to stretch, warm the body up with gentle jogging or skipping, for two to three minutes. Without that, there is a risk that you might pull a muscle doing the injury-preventing stretches!

Try to warm up all the major muscle groups taking the body through its full range of movements. Start with your legs and move up to the neck. Each position should be held for about ten seconds. Don't stretch the muscles to the absolute maximum – just to a point where you can feel a stretch without it being uncomfortable. Don't 'bounce' in any of the positions shown below either. The point of stretching is to improve the elasticity of the muscle; 'bouncing' can actually damage the elasticity without really stretching properly.

1

1) Keeping your heels on the floor, bend your knees and lean towards the wall. Hold for ten seconds. This stretches the lower calf area.

2) Straighten your left leg, bend the right, and lean forward, hands against the wall, so that your right leg is supporting your weight. Keep the heel of the left leg on the floor. Keep your toes in a straight line, pointing forward. This stretches the upper calf. Hold for ten seconds and then change legs.

2

3) Clasp your arms behind your legs, with your knees bent. Gradually lift your buttocks up until your legs are almost but not completely straight. This will stretch the hamstrings.

4

4) Clasping your right foot in your right hand, above the ankle, pull your right foot in towards your buttocks. Support your balance with your left hand, and keep your knees together. Change legs after ten seconds. This stretches the thigh muscles.

5

5) Stand with your legs wide apart, left foot pointing out, right foot facing forward. Bend the left knee, and take the body weight on the left leg, stretching the inside of the right thigh. Repeat for the right leg after ten seconds.

6

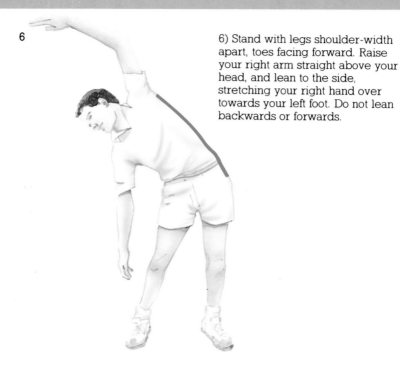

6) Stand with legs shoulder-width apart, toes facing forward. Raise your right arm straight above your head, and lean to the side, stretching your right hand over towards your left foot. Do not lean backwards or forwards.

7

7) Clasp your hands behind your back at hip level, and gently squeeze your shoulder blades together.

8) Hold your racket over the shoulder and hold the other end of it with your other hand. Move your hands closer together along the shaft of the racket, and hold for ten seconds.

9

9) Interlock hands above your head, and push the palms together. Hold for ten seconds.

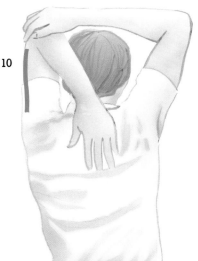

10

10) Hold your right arm aloft, elbow pointing up and hand down behind your neck. Hold right elbow with your left hand and gently squeeze the right arm back, stretching the triceps. Hold for ten seconds and change arms.

11

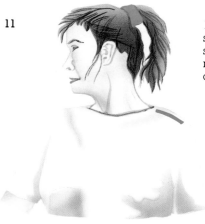

11) Look as far over your right shoulder as you can. Hold for ten seconds and repeat to the left. Do not move your head in complete circle, as this can be dangerous.

12) Lean your head to the right shoulder. Hold for ten seconds and repeat to the left.

12

13

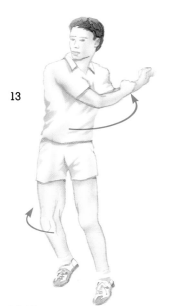

13) Finish your warm up with some more active exercise. Movement on a squash court involves a lot of twisting and turning, not just running in straight lines. Try 'dancing', twisting your hips and shoulders in opposite directions while bouncing on the spot.

14) Finally, run up and down the squash corridor, firstly forwards, lifting your knees high; then sideways, in both directions; then backwards. Now you are ready to go on court, and warm the ball up. This warm up should take five to eight minutes.

GLOSSARY

address   the position of the body at the point of impact
angle   a shot played to the front off the side wall – also called a boast
appeal   a player's request to the referee to consider an infringement
that may result in a let or a stroke being awarded. The correct form of
appeal is 'Let, please'. If there is no referee, the player may stop and
appeal in the same way to his opponent

backhand   the opposite direction of swing to that in which you would
normally throw a ball
backswing   the space taken by the racket in preparing for a shot
board   the lowest horizontal marking on the front wall of the court
boast   a shot played to the front off the side wall – also called an
angle

cross court   a shot played directly off the front wall to the side that is
furthest from the striker
cut line   the middle line on the front wall, six feet from the floor; the
service must go above it

down   the expression used to signify that a ball has hit the board or tin,
or has failed reach the front wall
drive   a direct shot to either back corner
drop   a soft shot to the front corner, directly off the front wall
downswing   the area of swing from the start of its downward journey
until the point of impact

follow through   the area of swing after impact with the ball
forehand   the direction of swing that corresponds with a natural
throwing action

game   part of a match, which starts with a service and ends with one
player reaching nine or ten points (in accordance with the rules)
game ball   the state of the score when the server requires one point to
win the game
ghosting   an exercise that involves moving to, and playing, a shot
without the ball

half court line   a line set on the floor parallel to the side walls, dividing
the back of the court into two equal parts and meeting the short line at its
midpoint to form the 'T'
hand   the period from the time a player becomes server until he
becomes receiver
hand out   the situation when a change of server occurs – a marker's call

kill   a hard hit shot to the nick

lob   a soft shot struck with enough height to clear the opponent and his
or her racket and finish in the back corner of the court

GLOSSARY

match ball   the state of the score when the server requires one point to win the match

nick   the corner between the side, or back, wall and the floor
not up   an expression used to indicate that a ball has not been hit in accordance with the rules, such as a service that does not go above the cut line or short line, or a ball that has bounced twice

out   the temr to indicate that a ball has hit the wall above the out line

point   a unit of the scoring system – a point is added to a player's score when he or she is server and wins a rally

racket face   the hitting surface of the racket
rally   a series of strikes of the ball – a rally commences with a serve and concludes when the ball ceases to be in play

service   the method by which the ball is put into play to start a rally
shadowing   going through the motions of a shot without the ball
short line   a line set out on the floor parallel to the front wall and 18 feet from it
straight shot   one played down the nearside wall
striker   the player whose turn it is to hit the ball after it has hit the front wall
stroke   the gain achieved by the player who wins a rally, either in the course of play or on award by the referee and which results in either the scoring of a point or change of hand

tin   the tin is situated between the board and the floor and is constructed in such a way as to make a distinctive noise when struck by the ball
trickle boast   a soft boast at the front of the court

volley   a ball that is struck before bouncing on the floor

THE RULES OF SQUASH

The rules of squash make complicated reading for the novice. Here is a short summary of the rules that you need to know before playing a game.

How to score

A match is the best of five games, that is the first person to win 3 games is the winner.

A game is to 9 points, unless the score reaches 8–8, when the receiver elects to play to 9 ('no set') or 10 ('set two').

Players have 1½ minutes rest between games.

Points can be scored only by the server. When the server wins a stroke, he or she scores a point. When the receiver wins a stroke, he or she becomes the server.

The score is always called with the server's score first.

How to serve

The right to serve first is decided by the spin of a racket.

The server must have at least one foot completely within the service box.

He must serve above the cut line, beyond the short line, and on the other side of the half court line to start the rally. The ball must also stay inside the 'out' line.

The server can choose which side to serve from. If the server wins the rally, he or she must change sides, and continue to do so until a rally is lost. When he or she regains service, the server can choose the side again.

The server has only one service.

Winning a rally

A rally ends when a player

(a) fails to return the ball above the board
(b) hits the ball out of court
(c) fails to hit the ball before the second bounce
(d) hits the opponent with the ball
(e) stops to ask for a let

Lets and strokes

A let is an undecided rally. The rally is replayed from the same side.

A stroke is a penalty point awarded if the striker is in a winning situation and there has been interference.

A player must make every effort to give his or her opponent a fair view of the ball and not to obstruct the opponent on his or her way to the ball.

Hitting your opponent

If you hit your opponent with the ball, and the ball was on a direct line to the front wall, a **stroke** is awarded.

If you hit your opponent with the ball and the ball was travelling to the side wall, a **let** is awarded.

If you 'turn' on the ball in the back corner and hit your opponent, even if the ball is travelling straight to the front, a **let** is again awarded.